THERE IS *L*IFE IN THE WORD!

PAUL E. COLLINS

ISBN 979-8-88685-629-3 (paperback)
ISBN 979-8-88685-630-9 (digital)

Christian Faith Publishing
832 Park Avenue
Meadville, PA 16335
www.christianfaithpublishing.com

Unless otherwise stated all Scripture is taken from the King James Version of the Bible.

Scripture quotations marked (NIV) are taken from the Holy Bible, New International Version®, NIV®. Copyright © 1973, 1978, 1984, 2011 by Biblica, Inc. ™ Used by permission of Zondervan. All rights reserved worldwide. www.zondervan.com The "NIV" and "New International Version" are trademarks registered in the United States Patent and Trademark Office by Biblica, Inc. ™

Scripture quotations marked (AMPCE) are taken from the Amplified Bible, Copyright© 1954, 1958, 1962, 1964, 1965, 1987 by The Lockman Foundation. Used by permission.

Printed in the United States of America

To my family. My late wife Ruth, son Paul, and precious daughter Candace: these are my compensation.

CONTENTS

PREFACE

The aim of this book is to provide information to the believer of Jesus Christ, nonbelievers, and one who may have strayed from Jesus concerning the heart, character, and intent of Almighty God. In the same way that one would test ride a vehicle and then come to a conclusion, this book serves the same purpose for the nonbeliever who may be in the valley of indecision concerning making Jesus your Lord and Savior, and for the believer looking for clarification in this area. I have included many passages of scripture that are intended to make clear the mind of God concerning His word and its purpose to all.

In the sixth chapter of Deuteronomy, verses 6 and 7, God instructs Moses to repeat much of what was previously stated in the earlier books of the Pentateuch by saying:

> And these words, which I command thee this
> day, shall be in thine heart: And thou shalt teach
> them diligently unto thy children, and shalt talk
> of them when thou sittest in thine house and
> when thou walkest by the way, and when thou
> liest down, and when thou risest up. (KJV)

That works out to be all the time. This practice carried on through the ages with the nation of Israel. One can plainly see that God intended for His word to be interacted as a lifestyle. When this discipline is implemented, God's word will reverberate through one's worldview and begin to grow and develop belief/faith in God and cut through and uproot strongholds of fear, inferiority complexes, rejection, and the like.

In the chapters that follow, you the reader are going to see the vital importance that the word of God plays, especially as it reveals the true and living God. That having been said, let's enter in.

ACKNOWLEDGMENTS

My wife is most deserving of thanks for providing a listening ear to my endless stream of thoughts and ideas and even providing feedback. Thanks, dear.

CHAPTER 1

Life in the Word

In the beginning was the word, and the word was with God, and the word was God. He was with God in the beginning. Through him all things were made; without him nothing was made that has been made. In him was life, and that life was the light of men...
The word became flesh and made his dwelling among us.
—John 1:1–4, 14a; New International Version

John was chosen to be a follower of Jesus and continued with the Master during his public ministry. After the death, burial, and resurrection of Jesus, John was inspired to write these words. He had a firsthand, eyewitness view of the word in action both during and after the ministry of Jesus. His being with Jesus does not necessarily qualify him for special recognition, but he being inspired by the word of God that resonated in his recreated human spirit does.

This is no snub toward Apostle John, nor do I intend to minimize his ministry in any way. I do, however, intend to weave a tapestry of the goodness of God via life in His word. King David writes in Psalms 107:20 in the King James Version:

He sent his word, and healed them, and delivered
them from their destructions.

David lived his life loving God and his word. He grew to become very familiar with and dependent upon God and his word; this qualified him to be a subject matter expert in this arena. He has seen firsthand how God can and has sent his word on many successful missions. Isaiah 55:8–11 in the King James reads as follows:

> For my thoughts are not your thoughts, neither
> are your ways my ways, saith the Lord.
> For as the heavens are higher than the earth,
> so are my ways higher than your ways, and my
> thoughts than your thoughts.
> For as the rain cometh down, and the snow from
> heaven, and returneth not thither, but watereth the
> earth, and maketh it bring forth and bud, that it
> may give seed to the sower, and bread to the eater:
> So shall my word be that goeth forth out of my
> mouth: it shall not return unto me void, but it shall
> accomplish that which I please, and it shall prosper
> in the thing whereto I sent it. (Isaiah 55:8–11)

Emphasis again is placed on God's living word's ability to fully accomplish their mission. I once heard Gloria Copeland, on the *Believers Voice of Victory* broadcast, say: "The word of God has the ability to bring itself to pass." What a profound statement. Jesus is recorded as saying in the Gospel of John 6:63, in the Amplified translation:

> It is the Spirit who gives life [He is the life-giver];
> the flesh conveys no benefit whatever [there is no
> profit in it]. The words (truths) that I have been
> speaking to you are spirit and life.

I happen to love Hebrews 4:12 in the Amplified; here's what it says:

> For the word that God speaks is alive and full
> of power [making it active, operative, energizing,

and effective]; it is sharper than any two-edged sword, penetrating to the dividing line of the breath of life (soul) and [the immortal] spirit, and of joints and marrow [of the deepest parts of our nature], exposing and sifting and analyzing and judging the very thoughts and purposes of the heart.

I want to park here. Notice the bracketed phrase above: "Making it active, operative, energizing, and effective." The writer of Hebrews is making an urgent appeal to his readers to allow the word of God to activate faith in God. He repeats this phrase in the fourth chapter of Hebrews: "Enter into his rest." The heart of God is exhorting His people, and anyone who hears, to abandon their fears, concerns, and fretting endeavors and trust in the One who is well able to fulfill his promises. Fear of the unknown, uncertainties, and agitating passions only lend itself to chaos. The God of the universe is highly concerned that we walk in the galvanizing certainty that He is with us and that He is true to His word. He urges you and me to grant His word access into our hearts, where it can effectively energize the operative and active power of God.

God is keenly aware of His ability, might, matchless power, and omnipotence. He also knows that when we abandon ourselves to His care and create a habitation for His word to abide and thrive, we then are in a much better position to participate and fellowship with Almighty God.

Our Heavenly Father God is a God of His word. The writer of Psalms said in 138:2 that Almighty God actually magnified His word above His very name! This is huge! If this is so, then how does God operate, what is His methodology, and what can we glean about Him from His word?

Let's address these questions in the next chapter.

CHAPTER 2

God's Modus Operandi!

In the book of Genesis, the book of beginnings, during God's masterful creation of the earth and all living things, God's mode of operation steps to the fore. In chapter one, the author notes the phrase "and God said" is usually followed by "And it was so." This was the case with the creation of light and with dividing the bodies of water from the water that comes from the skies. This was also true with the separation of the dry land from the seas, and with the formation of grasses, herbs, and trees that bears seeds for reproduction. The creation of lights—namely the sun and moon—for the purpose of dividing light from the darkness came about by the spoken words of God. He spoke and the waters brought forth life abundantly. He spoke yet again giving the directive to the earth to bring forth living creatures after their kind, and it was so.

On the sixth day according to verse 26:

> And God said, "Let us make man in our image, after our likeness: and let them have dominion over the fish of the sea, and over the fowl of the air, and over the cattle, and over all the earth, and over every creeping thing that creepeth upon the earth."

Much more follows between verses 26 and 30, but, in the latter part of verse 30, the phrase "and it was so" follows "Man became a living soul."

God is a God of faith; therefore He had and yet has total confidence in His spoken words. Clearly the creation of all things is directly attributed to the spoken words of the Almighty. There is a passage of scripture in the book of Hebrews that immediately comes to mind. It's found in the eleventh chapter and third verse:

> Through faith, we understand that the worlds
> were framed by the word of God so that things
> which are seen were not made of things which
> do appear.

Notice how the writer places God in the annals of faith!

The very appearance of Christ was a product of God's mode of operation. From the fall of man in Genesis to the book of Malachi, God spoke through his prophets of a coming one. These are known as messianic prophecies. Through these prophecies, Almighty God lays out the plan of redemption, the plan whereby mankind can be reunited with Him through His son, Jesus the Christ.

The first messianic prophecy came when man transgressed/violated the command of God and sinned. This particular action of disobedience separated man from God; separation from God is sin in its simplistic form. Father God actually created mankind for his pleasure; therefore, this separation can be seen as a devastating heart hurt to our loving Heavenly Father. The phrase "fall of man" implies the separation from the state of being vitally united to God. A state of existence, where the radiant glory of God pulsates through one's being, is synonymous with being vitally united or connected to God. God's creation was living the highest possible life where He was in constant contact and was a co-laborer with the creator of the universe. The fall of man also deprived him of his original state of dominion that was granted to him by God. Man knew no fear, no hurt, and no shortage of intelligence, no shortage of resources or mighty power.

Man was, in essence, one with God! This was designed by God for man.

I can see why an evil, jealous, and envious entity/devil can be so vitiated [debased] that he definitely would not want for any to enjoy these limitless wonders and exalted position. This explains why he designed such an ugly scheme of deception aimed at Eve. This access once belonged to him. This is a story for another time, but the dominion that was given to man was delivered to Satan by man. This may come as a surprise to some, but allow me to direct your attention to the passage of scripture where this originates.

Luke chapter 4 records Jesus being lead of the Spirit into the wilderness to be tempted of the devil. The devil, true to form, came to tempt Jesus in a number of ways. The weapon of choice used by Jesus was the Word, and this word put an end to the temptation! Take note of the words of the enemy in verse six:

> And the devil said unto him, "All this power will I give thee, and the glory of them: for that is delivered unto me; and to whomsoever I will I give it." (Luke 4:6)

I, for one, always assumed that he was lying until I noticed the response of Jesus in verse eight:

> Get thee behind me, Satan: for it is written, "Thou shalt worship the Lord thy God, and him only shalt thou serve." (Luke 4:8)

Notice that Jesus didn't deny. Father God immediately began to speak of a coming One who would redeem mankind back into loving favor, companionship, fellowship, and co-laboring with Him.

Once again, His mode of operation did not change. He began to speak in the book of Genesis 3:15 by saying:

> And I will put enmity between thee [Satan] and the woman, and between thy seed and her seed;

it shall bruise thy head, and thou shalt bruise his
heel.

He spoke two more times in Genesis, then in the book of
Deuteronomy, Psalms, and Isaiah many times. Micah, Haggai, and
Zechariah, and in Malachi 3:1, the Almighty says:

> Behold, I will send my messenger, and he shall
> prepare the way before me: and the Lord, whom
> ye seek, shall suddenly come to his temple, even
> the messenger of the covenant, whom ye delight
> in: behold, he shall come, saith the Lord of hosts.
> (Malachi 3:1)

The Almighty sent His word once again on a successful mission, and the Christ child arrived!

CHAPTER 3

Heart and Mouth

My son, attend to my words; consent and submit to my sayings.
Let them not depart from your sight; keep
them in the center of your heart.
For they are life to those who find them,
healing and health to all their flesh.
Keep and guard your heart with all vigilance and above all
that you guard, for out of it flow the springs of life.
—Proverbs 4:20–23 (Amplified Bible)

In the previous chapter, we saw that God's mode of operation was to speak what He believed in His heart. The reader of this passage is being encouraged to practice the discipline necessary for creating an abode in his or her heart, for the word to live, provide life, and be a blessing to others. To the man or woman who decides to take Jesus as Lord and Savior, there is an invitation, from God, to draw near to Him largely through word meditation. In so doing, we follow His example of heart and mouth agreement and qualify ourselves to participate with Him.

The word *heart* is used twice in this passage, found in both verses 21 and 23, and is of special significance. The word *heart* is used throughout the Bible and almost invariably refers to the inner-most being of man-his spirit. Apostle Paul refers to this as the *inward man* in 2 Corinthians 4:16.

This inward man is what is recreated into the image and likeness of God at the new birth or at salvation. The very life and nature of God come to live in us in our hearts! This new nature explains why one doesn't have the desires he or she once had. Vices have a way of falling off and losing the hold they once had.

In the book of Ezekiel, there are two passages that are strikingly similar. These two passages are actual prophecies spoken through Ezekiel. More specifically, these prophecies are utterances referred to as the gift of the word of wisdom. This particular gift of the Spirit of God often speaks of the plans and/or will of God. These utterances can also be instructions or specifics concerning people, places, or things that are futuristic in nature.

The first is found in chapter 36:25–27. Pay close attention to this plan of God; this very plan bespeaks [foretells] the unity of divinity with humanity.

> Then will I sprinkle clean water upon you, and ye shall be clean: from all your filthiness, and from all your idols, will I cleanse you. A NEW HEART also will I give you, and a new spirit will I put within you: and I will take away the STONY HEART out of your flesh, and I will give you a HEART OF FLESH. And I will put MY SPIRIT within you, and cause you to walk in my statutes, and ye shall keep my judgments, and do them. (Ezekiel 36:25–27)

Now compare this to chapter 11:19–20:

> And I will give them ONE HEART, and I will put a NEW SPIRIT within you; and I will take the STONY HEART out of your flesh, and will give them a HEART OF FLESH: That they may walk in my statutes, and keep mine ordinances, and do them: and they shall be my people, and I will be their God.

It is becoming more apparent, as we peer into the heart, character, and intent of the Almighty that He wants to interact, interface, and engage us to fellowship with His creation and to bathe us with His invigorating presence! What a good God we serve!

I will now return to the passage found in Proverbs 4:21–23 and tie some loose ends together.

In the preface, I referred to Deuteronomy chapter 6:6, 7 and noted that God's intent was for His people to make room for the message of His word to reverberate in their beings, in their hearts to come alive. This is a lifestyle that the Almighty is conveying. Now let us take a closer look at these passages and unearth some truths.

Verse 20 in the Amplified says:

> My son, attend to my words; consent and submit
> to my sayings.

According to the *Webster's New World Roget's A-Z Thesaurus*, being attentive is simply paying attention. Some of the synonyms used are these: observant, mindful, alert, and intent. The consent and submit is simply to obey God's words.

Verse 21 says:

> Let them not depart from your sight; keep them
> in the center of your heart.

These instructions parallel the instructions found in the Deuteronomy passage stated above. The message is clear; this practice/discipline is to be adopted as a lifestyle. This by no means is to be forced, perfunctory, or mechanical. One of my greatest joys is long study and meditation of the word of God.

Verse 22 gives one of the splendid benefits of doing so:

> For they are life to those who find them, healing
> and health to all their flesh.

This is consistent with the passage found in John 6:63:

> It is the Spirit who gives life [He is the life-giver];
> the flesh conveys no benefit whatever [there is no
> profit in it]. The words (truths) that I have been
> speaking to you are spirit and life.

If the Word promises healing, and it does, then when this word takes on life in one's heart/spirit, healing will be the result. If one battles with fear and meditates on passages that promise freedom from fear, then when that word begins to take root in one's heart, it will begin to uproot those ugly tentacles of fear and bring sweet freedom to the believer in Christ. The idea here is for the message communicated in a passage or passages to actually permeate one's worldview to the point where one becomes fully persuaded that what God has promised, He is also able to perform; this, my friend, is the process of building one's faith!

> Keep and guard your heart with all vigilance and
> above all that you guard, for out of it flow the
> springs of life. (Verse 23)

Matthew 12:34a is most telling in this instance for it reads:

> Out of the abundance of the heart the mouth
> speaketh.

In the above passages, the instructions are for the reader to make a lifestyle of ingesting the word of God [by way of study, mediation and reading], of really getting it deep in one's heart.

Eventually what goes into our hearts will come out in the form of words and actions. It, therefore, is of utmost importance that much care is taken to create a habitation for God's words so as to reap the benefits and to bless others with the life which issues forth from our hearts. Then our words that are full of faith are a benefit to others as well as to ourselves. There is life in the word of God!

I have made earlier references to the unity of divinity with humanity. The scriptures point to Father God reaching out to mankind with His plan of redemption. He has made many provisions for us to freely choose His providential care. The choice is ours. He will not force himself on any of us, and this also points to His care and fatherly way. Up to this point, I have touched on salvation but have not shown the very easy steps to actually carry it out. There are many scriptures that make clear the steps but the following are my favorite.

> But what saith it? The word is nigh thee, even in thy mouth, and in thy heart: [there is that heart and mouth agreement thing again] that is, the word of faith, which we preach; That if thou shalt confess [simply say] with thy mouth the Lord Jesus, and shalt believe in thine heart that God hath raised Him from the dead, thou shalt be saved. [It's just that simple]. For with the heart, man believeth unto righteousness; and with the mouth, confession is made unto salvation… For WHOSOEVER shall call upon the name of the Lord shall be saved. (Romans 10:8–10, 13, King James Version)

So here is how this plays out when in a church service where the word of God is being preached/taught, and the speaker gives the invitation [comes to the end of the sermon and asks if anyone wants to give their heart for the first time or rededicate their life to the Lord Jesus]; the speaker or a representative will have the candidates repeat something like this:

> Father God, come into my heart. Forgive me for my sins [actually this boils down to rejecting him by not accepting him sooner-many make the mistake of listing many acts of sin]. I believe that Jesus was sent to earth by you to take away my sin

and is the Son of God. I also believe that He died
for me and rose from the dead.

Believe this in your heart, and you are saved!
Your understanding of all the nuances may not be full but as
you continue in your quest of the Lord by the discipline of word
study and meditation, your understanding will grow.

Take the time to really ponder this; allow it to reverberate in
your thoughts for a time until it resonates in your being. By the way,
you are not confined to a church service; you can be in the quiet of
your home or in any place and make the decision.

CHAPTER 4

Obedience Is the Enabler!

I want to go back to the book of Deuteronomy and look at the heart, character, and intent of the Almighty. It is a very easy process to discern the character of a person by the things they say and by their actions. How very true of the Almighty.

In the passages that follow, Father God is preparing the nomadic nation of Israel for the conquest of the land that was promised to their ancestor Abraham. Reader, I do want you to understand that these scriptures are very much relevant to you today! You are probably not preparing to enter into a land mass for takeover, but you can rest assured that our Heavenly Father God has already provided the means of success in whatever you may be facing.

The nation of Israel were descendants of Jacob whose name was later changed to Israel, who were led out of Egyptian bondage by Moses. Once lead out of Egypt, they journeyed in the wilderness of Kadesh-barnea. At this particular time, Moses gathered this multitude by the river Jordan which borders the land of Canaan, the land that was promised to their ancestor Abraham many years before. They were gathered because Moses was about to give them instructions for their success in this new land. This information was none more than a large-scale recap of what was told to them, by God through Moses while in this wilderness. By the way, this large-scale recap was captured in five actual books written by Moses. It is known as *The Torah* or the five books of the law. In today's Bible, these are the first five books: Genesis, Exodus, Leviticus, Numbers, and Deuteronomy.

> Now therefore hearken, O Israel, unto the statutes and unto the judgments, which I teach you, for to do them, [now pay attention to God's reason for doing so] that you may live, and go in and possess the land which the Lord God of your fathers giveth you. (Deuteronomy 4:1)

Now let us consider verses 5 and 6.

> Behold, I have taught you statutes and judgments, even as the Lord my God commanded me, that ye should do so in the land wither ye go to possess it. Keep therefore and do them; [this next part really blesses me] for this is your wisdom and your understanding in the sight of the nations, which shall hear all these statutes, and say surely this great nation is a wise and understanding people.

Let's take a moment to reflect on what has been said. Father God wants for them to be equipped with the necessary tools for success in this new land. He wants for them to live in and to take ownership of their gift with a full understanding of what is to be done to succeed there as the head. He wants access into their lives by way of His living word, to be enabled to perform on their behalf. He knows that His living word had and has the necessary ingredients for them as well as for us today!

Deuteronomy 5:29, 33 goes on to say:

> O that there were such a heart in them, that they would fear me, and keep all my commandments always, [notice here that Father God intended for His Word to be interacted with as a lifestyle

and here's why] that it might be well with them, and with their children forever! This passage gives you the unique opportunity to peer into the heart and mind of the Almighty. [Now let's move on to verse 33] You shall walk in all the ways which the Lord your God hath commanded you, [please reader, take the time to ponder this next phrase] that ye may live, and that it may be well with you, and that ye may prolong your days in the land which ye shall possess.

Hear therefore, O Israel, and observe to do it; [again] that it may be well with thee, and [remember that Father God is speaking here] that ye may increase mightily, as the Lord God of thy fathers hath promised thee, in the land that floweth with milk and honey. (Deuteronomy 6:3)

Verses 24 and 25 are of particular interest.

And the Lord commanded us to do all these statutes, to fear the Lord our God, for our good always, that He might preserve us alive, as it is at this day. [This is the phrase of particular interest] And it shall be our righteousness, if we observe to do all these commandments before the Lord our God, as He hath commanded us.

Dear friend, there are many more passages of scripture that allow you to peer into the heart, character, and intent of the Almighty not only in the book of Deuteronomy but throughout the Bible! The more one reads studies and meditates upon the word of God, the clearer the message of God's love for the believer becomes. When this overall message permeates the mind and spirit/heart of the recipient, the easier it becomes to love, trust, and lean one whole reliance upon him hereby enabling him.

There is yet another phenomenon that evolves as one processes through the growth of his or her faith. Sarah, the wife of Abraham, learned firsthand just what I am conveying here. Father Abraham is billed as the father of faith. He indeed is, but Sarah is noted as having great faith as well and earned a place in the book of Hebrews' faith hall of fame! She learned that obedience to the word of God is indeed an enabler. It enables God to perform on our behalf as it did on hers: She was delivered of a child when she was past age because she judged Him faithful who had promised.

Notice the emphasis Father God places on the doing of His word in the above passages. He yearns for access into our affairs, but He will not force anyone to choose Him. He lists many benefits of diligence in the doing of His instructions. He is enabled to perform on our behalf when He is invited into one's heart through obedience and faith in Him and His word. The Almighty stands ready to show himself strong on the behalf of those whose heart is committed to him. King Solomon, the son of King David, is an excellent example of one who enabled God on his behalf. He was heir to the throne of David and he lacked the necessary wisdom to judge righteously.

Solomon grew up in a home where turbulence was no stranger. Sibling rivalry and war between a father and son are some of what he endured. He also witnessed a father who leaned the whole of his person on the true and living God of Israel. He experienced firsthand his father's faith in God, and as a result, he saw this same God do battle for his father. King David is known as one of history's greatest kings. Solomon, as a result, was mentored and groomed for kingly authority and for reliance upon God.

In First Kings chapter 2, the story opens with King David near death and admonishing his son to adhere to the commandments of the Lord. David well knew the secret of tapping into the stream of Godly success which was creating a habitation for God to dwell in one's heart and mind. He wanted his son to continue in the discipline of his fathers, as spelled out in Deuteronomy chapter 6, to fix one's gaze upon God's word, to the extent where its message really permeates one's heart, mind, and inner chambers of the personality. David's intent for his son was for the nutrients of God's nutrient-rich word to saturate his being to the point where it begins to speak to Solomon during his reign. This is the expectation of Father God today for His children; not a chore but a loving endeavor of interaction with Father God.

King David passes on and Solomon goes about his kingly duties following in the steps of his father. Chapter 3 and verse 3 finds King Solomon loved the Lord by heeding his father's very wise teachings and by obeying God's word. At this stage in his early career as king, Solomon is very concerned about judging righteously and wisely; he wants to lead the people of God in a manner that is pleasing to God.

Later in the same chapter, the Lord appears to Solomon in a dream and asks him what shall I give thee? This is a very critical juncture for Solomon because his actions, state of mind, and heart have appealed to God Almighty. Father God was very much enabled to perform on his behalf. If you are a nonbeliever, rest assured that if you make Jesus your Lord and Savior, and love Him by keeping His commandments/word, you too will indeed enable him in your affairs! If you are a believer and are looking for answers in this arena, attach your heart to loving Him in the same manner, and not only will you get to know Him better by judging the heart of the One Who said it, He will make Himself more fully known to you as well.

Now let us consider what Jesus has to say on this subject. In the Gospel of John, the writer records Jesus as pouring out His heart to His disciples because He is near the end of His earthly ministry and His life. The setting is the feast of the Passover which is one of the many feasts celebrated by the Jewish people. At the end of this celebration, Jesus decides to wash the feet of His disciples then He begins His farewell speech. One of the points He really emphasized was that loving Him was synonymous with [equal to] obeying His commands. The understanding being emphasized was that the Father would abide with them forever. Loving God is obeying Him and obeying Him enables Him.

There are two passages I want to present here, verses 21 and 23; both are found in the fourteenth chapter of John's Gospel from the Amplified Bible. These are marvelous passages!

> The person who has My commands and keeps them is the one who [really] loves Me, and whoever [really] loves Me [Please absorb what follows] will be loved by My Father, and I [too] will love him and will show (reveal, manifest) Myself to him. [I will let Myself be clearly seen by him and make Myself real to him.] (John 14:21, Amplified Bible)

In verse 23, Jesus answers a question by one of His disciples:

> Jesus answered, "If a person [really] loves Me, he will keep My word [obey My teaching]; and My Father will love him, [Again, please meditate on the following] and We will come to him and make Our home (abode, special dwelling place) with him."

In my estimation, the above two passages are benchmarks for the believer.

CHAPTER 5

Power, Confidence, and Might!

As the born-again believer [the one who accepts Jesus as Lord and Savior into their spirits/hearts] continues in the discipline of word study and meditation, the more one comes to know that Father God wants for His children to function in *His* power, confidence, and might! He truly wants for all of us to be galvanized as a result of spending time in His very strengthening presence!

I am a father of two very wonderful children who love the Lord and is doing very well. From time to time, I make it my business to tell them that they are my compensation. Parents have a way of feeling this way; I'm guilty. When they were young, I wanted very much for them to feel assured that if Mommy or Daddy were around, there was none to fear.

There are two passages of scripture that I like to link together in my study/meditation time. These really minister to me, so I'll spend time absorbing their message into my innermost being. The two passages are Psalms 91:1 and Ephesians 6:10 both found in the Amplified Bible.

Psalms 91:1 states the following:

> HE WHO dwells in the secret place of the Most High shall remain stable and fixed under the shadow of the Almighty [whose power no foe can withstand].

> In conclusion, be strong in the Lord [be empow-
> ered through your union with Him]; draw your
> strength from Him [that strength which His
> boundless might provides]. (Ephesians 6:10)

When I allow this message to reverberate in my thoughts and being, I become fortified with a sense of safety and well-being, much more than I was able to provide for my children.

What really adds meaning to this subject is the fact that Father God is with us. I am fully aware that in today's world, speaking of God in a Christian capacity has taken on a taboo slant. Many take on the role of the naysayer. In our country, Christianity seems to be very much under attack and seemingly on a collision course for extinction in our government.

However, nothing changes the fact that Father God is yet the Almighty, and no foe can stand before him in victory: He is the greatest of all! It is written that He will never leave or forsake us. He being with us is the very galvanization that all is and will be well. The sense of fearlessness and peace are the byproducts that follow this realization. Faith grows by leaps and bounds when the message in the above passages comes alive in our spirits! Let us consider some other passages that I have also meditated upon in times past that give substance.

In the first chapter of Joshua, the Lord speaks to him to reassure him of three things: That He is with him, of his mission, and even supplies the recipe for sure-footed success.

> There shall not any man be able to stand before
> thee all the days of thy life: [listen to the reason
> Father God gives Joshua]: as I was with Moses, so
> I will be with thee will not fail thee, nor forsake
> thee. (Joshua 1:5–9 in the King James)

Take note of the language of this upcoming phrase.

> Be strong and of a good courage: for unto this people shalt thou divide for an inheritance the land, which I sware unto their fathers to give them. [Also take notice of the part the word plays in the following] Only be thou strong and very courageous, that thou mayest observe to do according to all the law, which Moses my servant commanded thee: turn not from it to the right hand or the left, that thou mayest prosper whithersoever thou goest. This book of the law shall not depart out of thy mouth; but thou shalt meditate therein day and night, that thou mayest observe to do according to all that is written therein: for then thou shalt make thy way prosperous, and then thou shalt have good success.

The Lord closes with the following:

> Have not I commanded thee? Be strong and of a good courage; be not afraid, neither be thou dismayed: for the Lord thy God is with thee whithersoever thou goest.

If you read on in the book of Joshua, you will find that he performed many brave exploits because he was fully persuaded that what God had promised and God performed for him in a grand fashion. Prophet Isaiah was inspired to write these words by the Spirit of God in chapters 50:1–3:

> For the Lord God will help me; therefore shall I not be confounded: therefore have I set my face like a flint, and I know that I shall not be ashamed. He is near that justifieth me; who will contend with me? Let us stand together: who

is mine adversary? Let him come near to me. Behold, the Lord God will help me; who is he that shall condemn me? Lo, they all shall wax old as a garment; the moth shall eat them up. (Isaiah 50:1–3)

This is bold talk from major Prophet Isaiah. He experienced firsthand the strengthening agents found in the word of God, and we see the effects it had on him through his writings. Joshua, Isaiah, or any of the other writers of scriptures are no different than you or I; we can experience the same very tangible power, confidence, and might that God supply!

Now consider another passage found in Hebrews 5:5b, 6; which happens to have special significance to me:

For He hath said, I will never leave thee, nor forsake thee. So that we may boldly say, "The Lord is my helper, and I will not fear what man shall do unto me." (Hebrews 5:5b, 6)

When I was younger, I had my share of fear issues. I outgrew many of them but some remained into my adult life. As time progressed, I landed a job at a transportation company, and after meditating on this and other passages, I found myself very much at ease behind the wheel of either a sixty, forty, or thirty-five-foot bus; my mind would be on vacation, and I enjoyed a protected state during my years behind the wheel of those majestic vehicles.

I knew that Father God was true to His word. He is with every one of you who have made Jesus your Lord and Savior. He will be with each of you who decide to rededicate and/or commit your lives for the first time to Him and as you spend time in His presence; His presence will become more and more tangible. Now let us turn our attention to the New Testament and see what the Master has been recorded as saying on this subject.

At the end of the Book of Matthew, Jesus is commissioning [empowering and sending] His disciples to deliver the message of

Himself for the purpose of winning others to Himself; the message of salvation in other words.

Matthew is inspired to write this at the very end of verse 20 of chapter 28:

> And lo, I am with you always, even unto the end
> of the world.

The writer of the Gospel of Mark states this in verse 20 of chapter 16:

> And they went forth, and preached everywhere,
> the Lord working with them, and confirming the
> word with signs following. Amen.

The book of Acts of the apostles [formerly disciples] records many marvelous exploits of faith and marvels performed by the apostles as directed by the Holy Spirit of God [sent by Father God after the death, burial, and resurrection of Jesus]. They functioned with that trademark confidence, power, and might of God that Jesus did in His earthly ministry.

Apostle Paul was one such messenger that was mightily empowered by the Spirit of the living God in his day. He became saturated with the message of the scriptures to the point where he became a co-laborer with the Spirit of God.

One of the messages he pressed to get across to the believers was that Father God greatly desired for them to know the mighty power that was available to them. Paul lived in a time in history and in a region where the gospel message was less than acceptable.

He endured many perils as a result but was set ablaze with the power, confidence, and might of the Almighty. In his writings, Paul lists many of the sufferings he was subjected to by his own countrymen. Some were beatings, subjection to the elements, shipwrecked en route to a trial, and even imprisonment. As a matter of fact, he even wrote many of the epistles while in prison that we are blessed with today as a result.

On one occasion, Paul was inspired to write to a body of believers in Ephesus to the Ephesians' church. The actual message was a prayer. In this prayer, the heart of God Almighty shines forth in a manner which greatly blessed me. There is a yearning from the Master that is unmistakable!

I strongly encourage you to take the time to ponder, weigh and meditate on the passage found in Ephesians 3:14–21. In so doing, you open your spirit for its message to seed deep and to take on life so to live and demonstrate itself in your daily lives. The actual might of the Almighty will begin to reformat your worldview to the point where you begin to see through His lenses.

Those large looming, ugly, and long-lasting problems, i.e., giants, become smaller and not nearly as frightening as they once were. As a matter of fact, your perspective will take on the intended change [some call this a paradigm shift] so that they become insignificant bugs to be squashed in comparison to the Almighty!

This is how Jesus functioned in His earthly ministry. He was so saturated with the comforting truth that His Father God was with Him, that the enemy feared Him! This is what the Father expects of us: to operate in this life knowing that there is none to fear because He is near!

To further my point, the anger of the Lord was kindled against Moses! The Lord chose him to lead the nation of Israel out of Egyptian bondage, but he was afraid and offered the Lord many excuses. God told Moses certainly I will be with thee!

You can find this full account in the book of Exodus chapters 3 and 4. At the time, Moses was not convinced; eventually he went in the bold confidence of God. When Joshua was chosen next after Moses to lead the nation of Israel into the promised land, the Lord repeatedly emphasized to him to "Be strong and very courageous because as I was with Moses so will I be with you!"

There is a New Testament account of Jesus walking on the water toward a ship where His disciples were in a storm. Needless to say, this event scared the disciples for they thought He was a ghost. True to form, Jesus, reassured them that it was Him.

Peter said, "Lord, if it be you, bid me to come."

Jesus responded with, "Come."

Peter actually got out of the ship and walked on the water but took his eyes off of Jesus and directed his focus on those huge waves and began to sink! Jesus rescued him, and when they got on the ship, Jesus scolded Peter saying:

"O you of little faith, wherefore did you doubt?"

In each example I listed, these were people whose faith was groomed by God [Moses had a bit of a crash course], so more was expected of them. God works with all of us in the development of our faith just as we parents develop our children into adults.

Now for an examination of Ephesians' prayer in chapter 3:16–19 in the Amplified Bible, the whole prayer is captured in verses 14–21.

> May He grant you out of the rich treasury of His glory to be strengthened and reinforced with mighty power in the inner man by the [Holy] Spirit [Himself indwelling your innermost being and personality]. May Christ through your faith [actually] dwell (settle down, abide, make His permanent home) in your hearts! May you be rooted deep in love and founded securely on love. (Ephesians 3:16–19)

[Take the time to compare this message to the one found in John 14:21, 23.]

> That you may have the power and be strong to apprehend and grasp with all the saints [God's devoted people, the experience of that love] what is the breadth and length and height and depth [of it]: [That you may really come] to know [practically, through experience for yourselves] the love of Christ, which far surpasses mere knowledge [without experience]; that you may be filled [through all your being] unto all the fullness of

God [may have the richest measure of the divine presence and become a body wholly filled and flooded with God Himself]!

So what does this actually mean to you the reader? What can be gleaned from the above and what is Father God saying? In my conclusion I want to answer these with the following two points:

First, we can face any of life's problems knowing that we already have the victory.

Second, we then can function in a fearless capacity knowing that God is with us.

I once heard my spiritual father, Kenneth E. Hagin, say: "The crisis of life comes to all of us." How true this is! No one seems to be exempt from this reality. Even Jesus was subject to many challenges and even an ugly betrayal.

One thing that He communicated to His disciples and functioned in was the victory. He faced each challenge with the knowledge that He already had the victory. You then can face each of life's challenges, no matter how ugly or unfair, with the confidence of knowing that you are going to win. Situations have a way of coming hard, fast, and unannounced, and they can have a crippling hurting effect on one's heart,

But…the life in the word of God and His presence has a way of comforting and supplying a support system that not only eases the blows but fortifies us with the confidence of knowing that in the end, we win! Father wants each of us to function in this life with this benefit fully operational in our lives.

My second point is this: we can function in a fearless capacity knowing that God is with us. Some of us have experienced many of this life's ugly turns. These experiences have a way of leaving massive scars and trenches in the deep recesses of our memory like glaciers leave as they travel through landmasses. Often these show themselves as fears.

These fears can be triggered by unbeknownst actions of others. These fears have a way of haunting its host victim and robbing them of life's simple pleasures one of which is the fear that God is not with them or that He does not love or hear them. When the revelation of God's presence attaches to your spirit, these agitating things lose their hold; they begin to move away as if in terror.

Your outlook on life can change, and you will face fears with the undaunted knowing that they must move out! This is the power of confidence and might the Father expected the Bible characters to operate in as a matter of course.

This is the power, confidence, and might that are yours to function in as well. This is one of the many gifts and benefits that await the man or woman that makes God their Lord and Savior.

Be blessed in the name of Jesus.

About the Author

Paul E. Collins, a United States Army Veteran of eight years, began his ministry with his late wife Ruth C. Collins in June of 1990 after receiving the baptism of the Holy Spirit. From 1990 to the early 2000s, Paul and Ruth were involved in a number of ministry roles and projects all of which were most rewarding but most notably a healing ministry entitled the Healing Team.

Paul and Ruth both received ministry credentials from the Pittsburgh-based Greater Works Outreach school of ministry. Since then, Paul went on to achieve a baccalaureate in human resources and an MBA and is now happily retired from public service.